Mercury

Revised Edition

by Steven L. Kipp

Consultant:
Gregory L. Vogt
Teaching from Space Program
Oklahoma State University

Bridgestone Books
an imprint of Capstone Press
Mankato, Minnesota

Bridgestone Books are published by Capstone Press
151 Good Counsel Drive, P.O. Box 669, Mankato, Minnesota 56002
http://www.capstone-press.com

Library of Congress Cataloging-in-Publication Data
The Library of Congress has cataloged the first edition as follows:
Kipp, Steven L.
    Mercury/by Steven L. Kipp.
    p. cm.—(The galaxy)
    Includes bibliographical references and index.
    Summary: Discusses the orbit, surface features, exploration, and other aspects of the
planet Mercury.
    ISBN 0-7368-0518-4
    1. Mercury (Planet)—Juvenile literature. [1. Mercury (Planet)] I. Title. II. Series.
QB611.K57 1998
523.41—dc21

                                                                          97-6918
                                                                          CIP

Editorial Credits
Tom Adamson, editor; Timothy Halldin, cover designer and illustrator; Kimberly Danger
    and Jodi Theisen, photo researchers

Photo Credits
NASA, cover, 1, 8, 10, 12, 14, 16, 20
New Mexico State University Observatory, 18
Steven L. Kipp, 6

1 2 3 4 5 6 05 04 03 02 01 00

Table of Contents

Relative size of the Sun and the planets

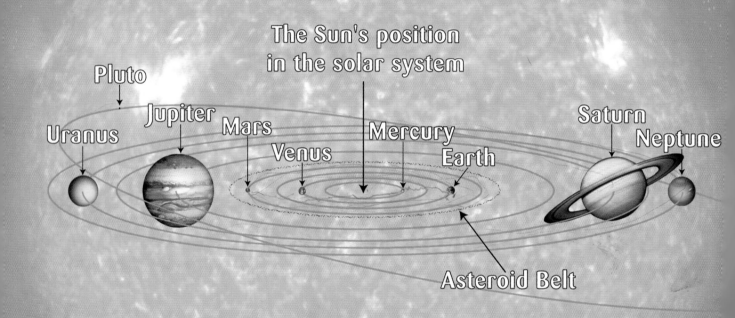

The Sun's position
in the solar system

Pluto

Uranus

Jupiter

Mars

Venus

Mercury

Earth

Saturn

Neptune

Asteroid Belt

The Sun

Mercury is a planet in the solar system. The Sun is the center of the solar system. Planets, asteroids, and comets travel around the Sun.

Mercury is the closest planet to the Sun. Mercury is about 36 million miles (58 million kilometers) away from the Sun. Mercury is one of four inner planets that have rocky surfaces. Venus, Earth, and Mars are the other inner planets. Jupiter, Saturn, Uranus, and Neptune are the outer planets. These giant planets are made of gases.

Pluto is made of rock and ice. Pluto is the only planet that is smaller than Mercury.

◀ **This illustration compares the sizes of the planets and the Sun. Mercury is the second smallest planet. The blue lines show the orbits of the planets. Mercury is the closest planet to the Sun. Thousands of asteroids move around the Sun. The asteroid belt is between the orbits of Mars and Jupiter.**

Mercury is 3,031 miles (4,878 kilometers) wide. Almost 18 planets the size of Mercury could fit into one Earth.

In the past, people thought Mercury was really two planets. Mercury sometimes appears in the eastern sky before sunrise. Other times, it appears in the western sky after sunset. People later learned that it was the same planet.

Mercury is hard to see from Earth. The planet is always near the Sun in the sky. The bright light of the Sun makes Mercury hard to see. Mercury is visible just before sunrise or just after sunset. The Sun's light does not hide Mercury during these times.

Mercury is visible in this picture taken just after sunset.

FAST FACTS

	Mercury	Earth
Diameter:	3,031 miles (4,878 kilometers)	7,927 miles (12,756 kilometers)
Average distance from the Sun:	36 million miles (58 million kilometers)	93 million miles (150 million kilometers)
Revolution period:	88 days	365 days, 6 hours
Rotation period:	59 days	23 hours, 56 minutes
Moons:	0	1

The Hot and Cold Planet

Most planets have an atmosphere. This mixture of gases forms a layer around a planet. The atmosphere holds in heat from the Sun. Mercury has almost no atmosphere. Mercury's gravity is too weak to keep the gases around the planet. The gases escape into outer space.

Without much atmosphere, Mercury has extreme temperatures. The side of Mercury that faces the Sun is very hot. The temperature reaches 800 degrees Fahrenheit (430 degrees Celsius). This temperature is 300 degrees hotter than most ovens can reach.

The side of Mercury that faces away from the Sun becomes very cold. The temperature can drop to minus 300 degrees Fahrenheit (minus 180 degrees Celsius).

Liquid water cannot exist on a planet with these temperatures. But scientists think they have found water ice inside craters at Mercury's poles. Sunlight never shines into these craters. The ice never melts.

The gravity on Mercury is weak. This force is not strong enough to pull gases into the planet's atmosphere.

core

crust

Magnetic Field

The outer part of Mercury is called the crust. The crust is made of solid rock. The solid rock floats on the liquid metal of the core.

The core is the center of Mercury. This part of the planet is more than 2,230 miles (3,600 kilometers) thick. The core is made of rock and iron.

Mercury's core creates a magnetic field around the planet. This force surrounds magnets. Liquid metal in the core acts like a magnet. Mercury does not have much liquid metal, so its magnetic field is very weak. The field does not shield Mercury from electrically charged particles from the Sun.

Earth also has a magnetic field. Earth has more liquid metal in its core than Mercury. Its magnetic field is larger than Mercury's. Earth's magnetic field protects the planet from the Sun's harmful charged particles.

Mercury has a large core compared to its size.

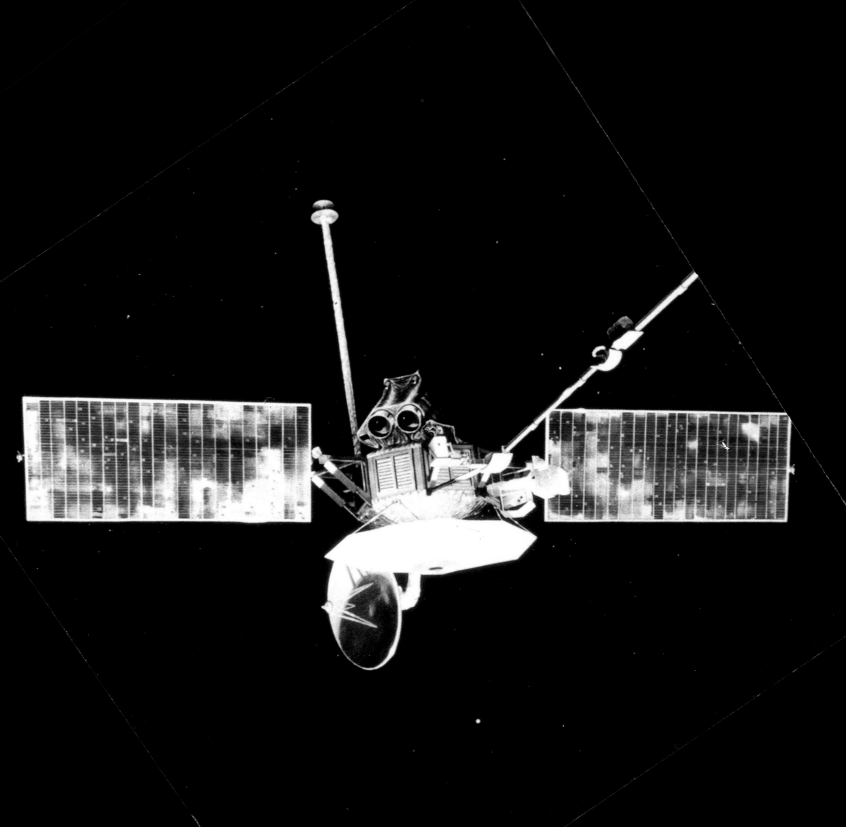

Mariner 10

Telescopes help scientists learn about Mercury. A telescope makes faraway objects look larger and closer. But Earth's atmosphere and the Sun's light make Mercury difficult to see. Scientists cannot see the planet's surface features with telescopes.

Scientists send space probes to other planets to study them more closely. The *Mariner 10* space probe helped scientists learn about Mercury's surface. *Mariner 10* flew past Mercury in the 1970s.

Mariner 10 sent pictures of Mercury's surface to Earth. These pictures showed that many craters cover Mercury. Asteroids and comets crashed into the planet and made the craters. Asteroids are large space rocks that orbit the Sun. Small pieces of an asteroid that crash onto a planet's or a moon's surface are called meteorites. Comets are large chunks of ice and dirt that orbit the Sun. The ice at Mercury's poles could have come from comets.

The space probe *Mariner 10* took pictures of Mercury.

Early Romans named Mercury. All planets except Earth are named for characters in Greek and Roman myths. In these ancient stories, Mercury was the messenger for the gods. This symbol stands for the planet Mercury.

The largest feature on Mercury is the Caloris Basin. A basin is a very large crater. Basins and craters are wide and usually shallow. The Caloris Basin is about 800 miles (1,300 kilometers) wide.

Astronomers think a giant asteroid made the Caloris Basin when it crashed into Mercury. The powerful crash made mountains. These mountains surround the Caloris Basin. The crash also formed hills on the other side of the planet.

Mercury also has large splits on its surface. The splits are so large that pieces of land dropped into them. This movement formed cliffs called scarps. Some scarps stretch for long distances across Mercury's surface.

Some craters have bright rays extending from them. Astronomers think that these craters are not as old as other craters. But scientists believe that Mercury's surface has not changed for hundreds of millions of years.

Mercury's surface has many craters and scarps.

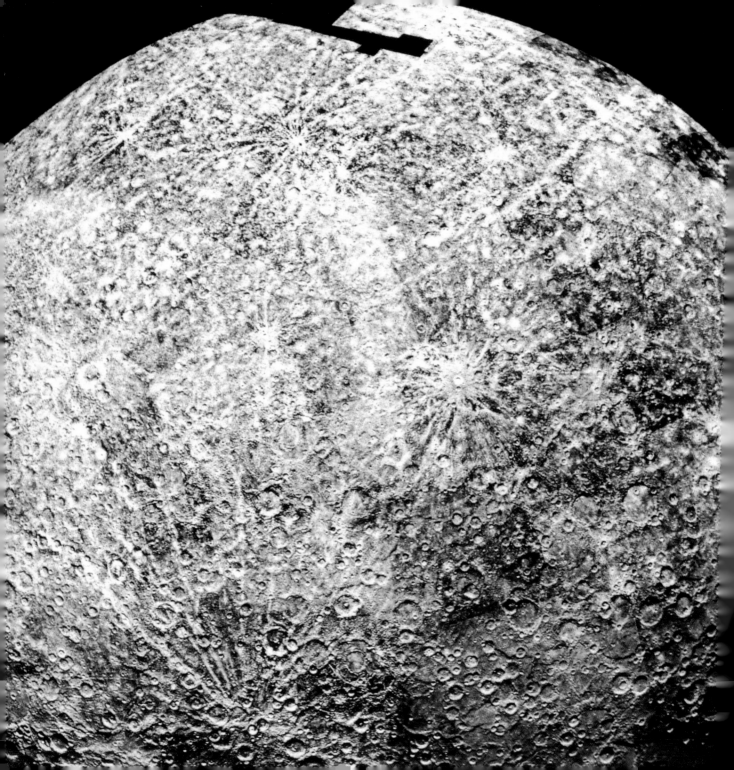

Revolution and Rotation

Like all other planets, Mercury orbits the Sun. One complete orbit is called a revolution. Mercury makes one revolution every 88 days. Mercury orbits the Sun faster than any other planet. One year on Mercury is 88 days long.

Mercury also rotates, or spins, as it orbits. Mercury rotates slowly. The planet makes one rotation every 59 days. Mercury rotates one and one-half times during each revolution. The planet rotates three times every two trips around the Sun.

Mercury's revolution and rotation speed help scientists measure its solar day. The solar day is the time from one sunrise to the next sunrise. Mercury's solar day is equal to 176 days on Earth.

To someone standing on Mercury, the Sun would appear in the sky for 88 days. After sunset, the sky would be dark for 88 days.

The parts of Mercury that the Sun lights become very hot.

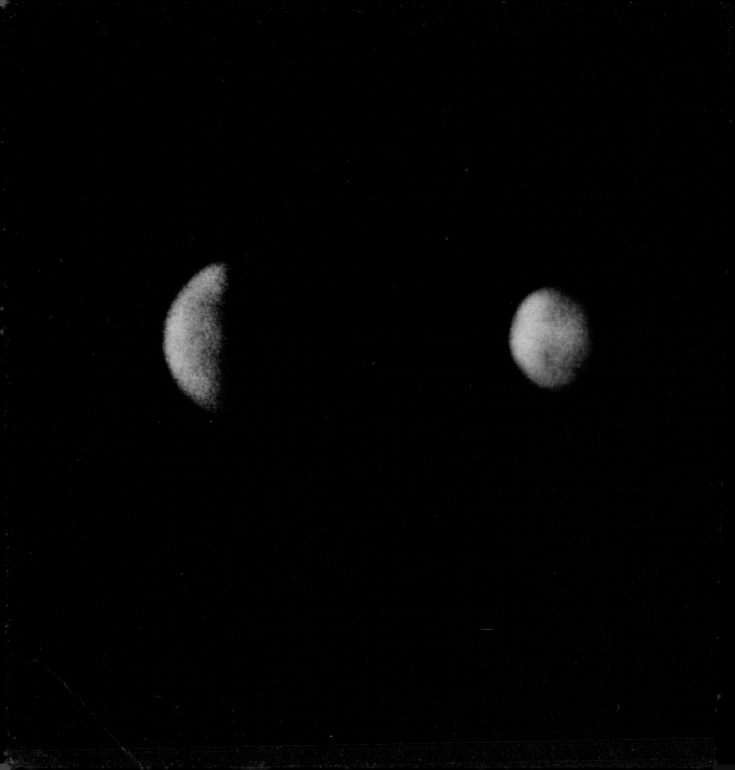

People who watch Mercury with a telescope see that the planet seems to change shape. But Mercury does not really change shape. The Sun lights different parts of the planet as it travels in its orbit.

From Earth, people see only the part of Mercury that the Sun lights. The part that people see is called a phase.

Mercury sometimes passes between the Sun and Earth. This movement is called a transit. People can see transits of Mercury only with special telescopes. These telescopes filter out the Sun's bright light. During a transit, Mercury looks like a small dot moving across the Sun. The next transit of Mercury will happen on May 7, 2003.

These pictures show two phases of Mercury. People can see only the part of the planet lit by the Sun.

The *Mariner 10* space probe mapped about half of Mercury's surface. Scientists have learned much about Mercury. But they still have many questions. They want to learn more about Mercury's magnetic field and core. They also hope to find out if there is ice at Mercury's north and south poles.

In 2004, scientists plan to send the space probe *MESSENGER* to Mercury. This spacecraft will fly past the planet Venus twice. The space probe will fly past Venus in 2006 and again in 2007. It will then fly close to Mercury in 2008. *MESSENGER* will begin to orbit Mercury in 2009. With this mission, scientists hope to solve some of the planet's mysteries.

Scientists had to put together several pictures from *Mariner 10* to make this larger view.

Hands On: Make Craters

Small and large craters cover Mercury's surface. Meteorites formed the craters when they crashed into the planet. You can make your own craters with mud and pebbles.

What You Need

An empty pie plate
Mud
Pebbles and small rocks

What You Do

1. Fill the pie plate with mud.
2. Carefully drop some pebbles and small rocks on the mud.
3. Leave the pebbles and rocks in the mud. Let the mud dry for several hours.
4. Remove the pebbles and rocks. Craters have formed in the mud.

The mud is like the surface of Mercury. The pebbles and rocks are like the meteorites that crashed into Mercury. You removed the pebbles and rocks yourself. But the real meteorites that crashed into Mercury exploded into small pieces.

Words to Know

asteroid (ASS-tuh-roid)—a large space rock that orbits the Sun

astronomer (uh-STRON-uh-mer)—a person who studies planets, stars, and space

basin (BAY-suhn)—a very large crater

crater (KRAY-tur)—a hole in the ground made by a meteorite

gravity (GRAV-uh-tee)—a force that pulls objects together

meteorite (MEE-tee-ur-rite)—a piece of space rock that strikes a planet or a moon

phases (FAZE-ess)—the different parts of a planet or a moon lit by the Sun

revolution (rev-uh-LOO-shuhn)—the movement of one object around another object in space

rotation (roh-TAY-shuhn)—one complete spin of an object in space

scarp (SKARP)—a cliff formed by splits in a planet's surface

space probe (SPAYSS PROHB)—a spacecraft that travels to other planets and outer space

Read More

Brimner, Larry Dane. *Mercury*. A True Book. New York: Children's Press, 1998.

Kerrod, Robin. *Astronomy*. Young Scientist Concepts and Projects. Milwaukee: Gareth Stevens, 1998.

Simon, Seymour. *Mercury*. New York: Mulberry Books, 1998.

Useful Addresses

Canadian Space Agency
6767 Route de l'Aéroport
Saint-Hubert, QC J3Y 8Y9
Canada

NASA Headquarters
Washington, DC 20546-0001

The Planetary Society
65 Catalina Avenue
Pasadena, CA 91106-2301

Internet Sites

MESSENGER Online
http://sd-www.jhuapl.edu/MESSENGER/index.html
Let's Explore the Nine Planets
http://www.staq.qld.edu.au/k9p/title.htm
StarChild
http://starchild.gsfc.nasa.gov/docs/StarChild/
StarChild.html

Index